The Earth
is like a
roundabout

First published in Great Britain in 1999 by Macdonald Young Books

Macdonald Young Books,
an imprint of Wayland Publishers Ltd
61 Western Road
Hove, East Sussex
BN3 1JD

Text © Claire Llewellyn 1999
Illustrations © Anthony Lewis 1999
Volume © Macdonald Young Books 1999
M.Y.Bees artwork © Clare Mackie

Commissioning Editor: Dereen Taylor
Editor: Lisa Edwards
Designer: Rebecca Elgar
Language Consultant: Betty Root
Science Consultant: Georgina Hooper

A CIP catalogue for this book is available from the British Library

Printed and bound in Portugal by Edições ASA

ISBN 0 7500 2644 8

The Earth is like a roundabout

Claire Llewellyn

Illustrated by
Anthony Lewis

MACDONALD YOUNG BOOKS

The Earth is like a roundabout.

It turns round and round and round.

6

It keeps on turning, it never slows down...

...and it certainly never stops.

7

The Earth spins quickly, but you never feel it –

Far away in the darkness of space, other planets are spinning too. Some of them rush round, but others take their time.

The planets move round the scorching Sun, which burns like a huge bonfire.

Where it shines on the Earth, there's warmth and light.

Where it doesn't, there's inky-black night.

13

The turning Earth spins us around through the night to face the Sun and a brand-new day.

14

15

Days are for doing things.
They are for working...

...and talking...

...and learning.

16

They are for growing...

...and feeding...

...and caring for the young.

17

But hour by hour, the roundabout Earth
turns us away from the Sun. The sky
grows darker and the air feels cool.

What's happening
in the garden now?

19

The spinning Earth carries us into the night. For most of us it's time to sleep.

20

But on the other side of the roundabout,

it's the start of another day.

Night after day, day after night,
we move from the light to the dark.

In cities,

in deserts,

on islands,

and in forests.

25

This is the pattern of the lives we lead...

...on our home the roundabout Earth.

The Spinning Earth

A roundabout turns on an upright pole, but the Earth turns slightly on its side. The Earth doesn't turn on a real pole. It has an imaginary one, called an axis. The ends of this axis are called the North and South Poles.

North Pole

South Pole

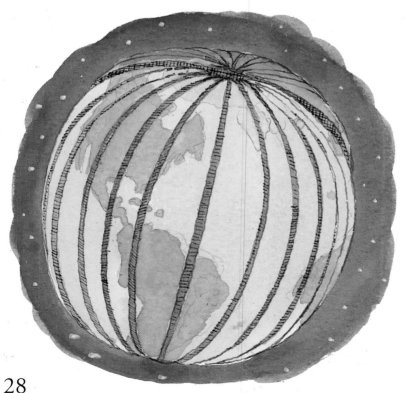

The Sun rises and sets at different times around the Earth. Because of this, clocks and watches around the world tell completely different times. To help us keep track of time, the world has been split up into 24 time zones. There is one for every hour of the day.

The Sun in the Sky

During the day, the Sun seems to move across the sky. But it's not the Sun that's moving it's the Earth. In the morning, we're turning towards the Sun. We see it first in the east. This is called sunrise.

By midday, we're directly facing the Sun. It is high above us in the sky.

In the evening we're turning away from the Sun. We see it sink down in the west. This is called sunset.

GLOSSARY

Desert

A dry place where there is very little rain.

Island

A piece of land with water all around it.

Planet

A large, round object in Space that moves round a star. The Earth is one of nine planets that move round the Sun.

Space

Everything that lies outside the Earth.

Star

A spinning ball of gas which gives off huge amounts of heat and light. A star can be seen as a tiny point of light in the sky at night.